Stroke your kitten
to make it purr!

When your kitten gets hungry, **make sure you give it plenty of delicious food.**

Kittens love to play.
Choose a toy for your kitten
and join in the fun!

D1247288

View each page in the app to find fun new kitten activities!

★★★★★

THIS IS A CARLTON BOOK

Published in 2018 by Carlton Books Limited, an imprint of the Carlton Publishing Group, 20 Mortimer Street, London WIT 3JW

Text and design copyright © Carlton Books Limited 2018

A catalogue record for this book is available from the British Library.

ISBN: 978-1-78312-422-0

Printed in China

1 3 5 7 9 10 8 6 4 2

Written by: Kay Woodward
Executive Editors: Stephanie Stahl and Joff Brown
Design Manager: Emily Clarke
Design: Ceri Hurst
Picture research: Paul Langan
Production: Nicola Davey

★★★★★

The publishers would like to thank the following sources for their kind permission to reproduce the pictures in this book.

T=top, B=bottom, C=centre, L=left, R=right.

Shutterstock: /Africa Studio: 9TR; /Vasilyev Alexandr: 5TL, 30TL; /Poprotskiy Alexey: 28TL; /Utekhina Anna: 5C, 10C; /Atmosphere1: 18C; /bswhitfield: 7TR (fur 1); /Oksana Bystritskaya: 24TL; /Tony Campbell: 29TR; /Victor Dyatlov: 26BR; /CebotariN: 26TL; /Chendongshan: 5BR, 22C, 32BL; /Cherry-Merry: 30R; /De Jongh Photography: 7TR (fur 2); /Gornostay: 8R; /Mark /Valeska Engel: 21TR; /Evdoha_spb: 7TR (fur 4); /Foonia: 4TR, 16TL, 32TR; /Sergey Gerashchenko: 7BR; /My Agency: 19T, 32BR; /Natalia7: 14R; /Hayes: 11L; /Andrey_Kuzmin: 20R; /LesiChkall27: 6R; /Lubava: 25TR; /MaraZe: 15BR; /Pattern image: 7TR (fur 6); /Anurak Nenov Brothers Images: 24C; /Okssi: 16C; /Alena Ozerova: 1BL, 18TL; /Ronnachai Palas: 7BL; /Seregraff: 12C; /Nolha Shaukavets: 17R; /Smit: Pongpatimet: 1TR, 12TL, 22TL; /Alena Rozova: 27TL; /Lev Savitskiy: 7TR (fur 5); /taratynova.photo: 28BR; /The Len: 8TL, 32TL; /Albina Tiplyashina: 4TC, 14TL; 1TL, 6TL; /stalk: 23TL; /Roman Stetsyk: 7TR (fur 3); /Camil Zahner: 20TL; /Dora Zett: 13BL /vvita: 10TL; /WilleeCole Photography: 24R;

'Lola' from Audrey Hazell-Graham: 1BR, 4TL

Every effort has been made to acknowledge correctly and contact the source and/or copyright holder of each picture and Carlton Books Limited apologises for any unintentional errors or omissions, which will be corrected in future editions of this book.

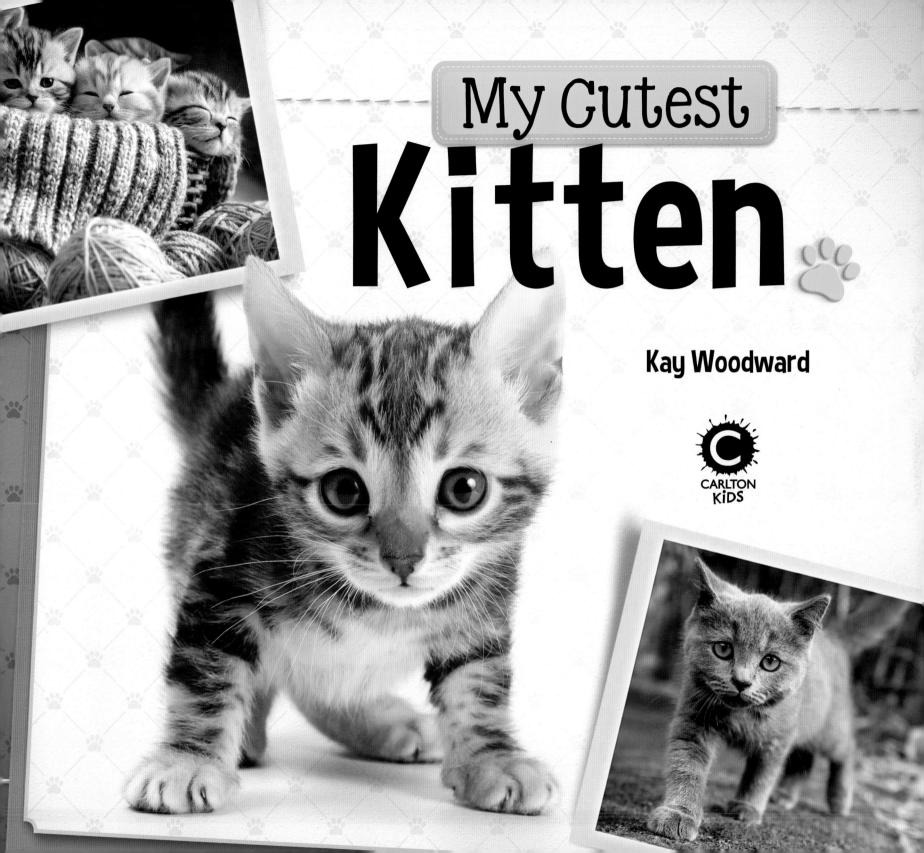

My Cutest Kitten

Kay Woodward

CARLTON KIDS

IT'S KITTEN TIME!

Kittens aren't just sweet. They're the most amazingly cute and super adorable creatures ever! It's impossible to look at one and *not* say, 'Awwwwwww.' But what if you could have the cutest kitten of all...? Guess what? You *can*.

This kitten could be yours!

SURPRISE!

In real life, you can't choose your kitten... your kitten chooses you. Your kitten might be a striped tabby or a tortoiseshell. It could be as black as night or as white as snow. Or ginger or grey or cream or brown or cinnamon or fawn or a mixture of colours! But in Augmented Reality, you get to choose your kitten's eye and fur colour. So trigger the app and get ready to meet the cutest kitten you ever saw.

A KITTEN CALLED...

The first thing your new kitten needs is a name. Will you choose something sweet like Magic, something fun like Mischief, or something practical like Trevor? Friends and family might suggest names, but remember that this is *your* kitten. If you just love the name Smudgywudge, then go for it. The choice is 100% yours.

Oh, I do hope my name is Einstein...

YOUR OWN KITTEN

★ ★ ★ ★ ★

Choose your kitten's fur and eye colour, and meet your new best friend!

FUR COLOURS

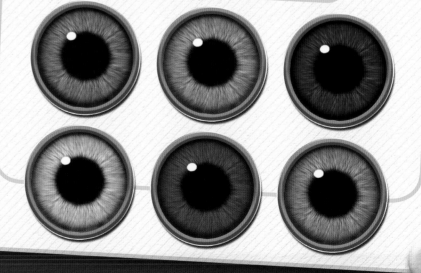

EYE COLOURS

HELLO, KITTY!

Just because they're cute and furry doesn't mean kittens and puppies are the same. They're *really* not. So if you're already an expert in puppy behaviour, then prepare to forget everything. It's time to greet your kitten in an entirely new way...

So, you think you know kittens? Think again.

SLOWLY, SLOWLY...

Kittens are so completely loveable that you probably feel like smothering yours with cuddles right away. But stop right there. Kittens like to get to know *you* first. Hold out your hand and let the kitten come to you. If it just stares at you, then try again later. It's clearly not in the mood. But if the kitten rubs its face against your hand, then it's OK to pet them, very, very carefully.

I'm so pleased you're my new owner!

ATTENTION!

If a kitten rolls on its back, this is kitten code for: *please, please, please stroke me. Pay me some attention right now.* So go for it! Try gently massaging the top of the kitten's head or petting its cheeks. You could even stroke the kitten from forehead to tail. If it likes something, the kitten will nudge your hand to make you do it again. If it doesn't, the kitten will put her ears back or simply walk away.

Never stroke a kitten from its tail to its forehead. Some of them really, really don't like it.

KITTEN CUDDLES ★★★★★

★★★★★

Stroke your cuddly kitty and you'll make a friend forever!

I'm seriously rocking this look!

COOL FOR CATS

Would you like your new pet to be the envy of the cat world? Excellent. Because it's time to pick the purr-fect collar and a meow-vellous nametag to hang on it.

COLLAR

Different collars suit different kittens, so pick one that matches your pet's character. What's your kitten like? If it looks like a mischievous bundle of fun, then the kitten might suit a bright orange collar. But if it looks as if they'd be happiest creeping stealthily along the top of a wall like a spy, then perhaps a dark blue collar is for them!

I'm really not sure if this collar suits me.

NAMETAG

Cats love to roam. So by giving your kitten a nametag as soon as possible, you'll be doing it a huge favour. If it ever gets lost, you'll soon be reunited. Simply choose the shape and colour of the nametag you like best. Once you've decided, it will magically appear on your kitten's collar!

KITTEN STYLE
★ ★ ★ ★ ★

Your best friend will look super fashionable with these fabulous accessories!

Pick your favourite nametag...

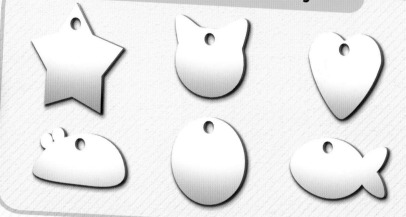

...then choose a collar for your cutest kitten.

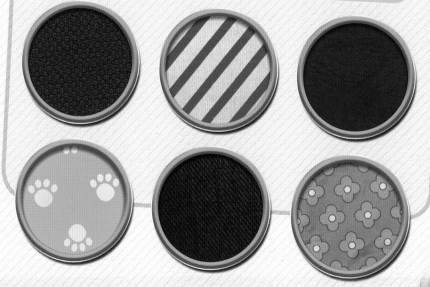

KITTEN FUN!

Geronimo!

What do kittens want? Fun! When do they want it? Now! Your furry friend can't wait to run and leap and pounce. This is how kittens learn. They're mastering the moves that they will need when they are older and wiser cats.

There's a very good reason why I do this, but I'm not telling you!

KITTEN-GO-ROUND

Have you ever seen a kitten whizz round and round in circles? It isn't trying to make itself dizzy – it's chasing its own tail! (Sometimes, the kitten even catches its tail! And then it lets it go again, because otherwise it would be really tricky to walk.) So why does a kitten do this? Maybe it's because it's practising chasing prey, so it will be a top hunter when it's older? Or perhaps it's just THE BEST FUN EVER. Who knows? (The kitten, of course.)

A FURRY TAIL

If you've ever wondered how a kitten is feeling, their tail is the key! It reveals all sorts of secrets about the kitten's moods. A tall, straight tail shows that your kitten is happy. If it's curved, the kitten wants to play! But if the kitten's tail is very low or – even worse – if it's whipping from side to side, then WATCH OUT. The kitten is very, very angry indeed.

LET'S PLAY!

★ ★ ★ ★ ★

What your cuddly friend really loves is leaping, chasing its tail or even rolling over onto its back.

PICK A GAME

Are you ready to play with your kitten? Fabulous! Because guess what? Your pretty pet can't wait to play with you! It's the perfect way to bond with your kitten and it's a wonderful way for them to exercise too. (It also stops them climbing the curtains.)

Let's play hide-and-seek!

I'm quite easy to please, you know.

TOYS

Cats don't need complicated toys. They're deliriously happy with these everyday objects.

1. **A ball of string.**
   Yes, really. It's not a myth. Give your kitten a ball of string and they'll be beyond happy!

2. **A scrunched-up ball of paper.**
   This is not just fun to play with. It makes a lovely crinkly, crackly, crunchy sound, too!

READY, SET... FUN!

★ ★ ★ ★ ★

Your kitten will love playing with this marvellous mouse toy.

CAT AND MOUSE

In cartoons, cats love to chase mice. But did you know that your kitten can have just as much fun scampering after a toy mouse? It's great exercise and will make sure that by the time it's a fully grown cat, your kitten's hunting skills will be tip-top. Tie a toy mouse to a piece of string, then tug the mouse away. The kitten will be chasing and pouncing in no time!

Watch out! This time, I'm going to catch you!

MMM...

Kittens grow very, very quickly. When they are just a few weeks' old, they may weigh twice as when they are born! They are also super active. So kittens need lots of food to give them oodles of energy for growing and playing.

I'm super hungry!

Kittens prefer to eat a few small meals throughout the day rather than one enormous feast.

NICE... AND NAUGHTY

At first, kittens drink their mother's milk. But they are soon ready to munch on meaty meals. Top kitten treats are cooked eggs, cooked fish and cucumber. Yum! Yum!

FOOD, GLORIOUS FOOD

The best food for a kitten is... kitten food! It's packed with the protein that growing kittens need. And because it's hard to squeeze enough goodness into one meal, kittens gobble three or four meals every single day. As they grow older, they need just two meals a day.

BON APPETIT!

Pick a meal to feed your kitten and see if it likes it.

 TOP TIP

Once they finish drinking their mother's milk, kittens don't drink milk (it gives them upset tummies!) Only give your kitten water to drink.

SLEEPY KITTENS

Newborn kittens snooze for nearly 22 hours a day! As they grow older they need less sleep, but a six-month-old kitten still needs to nap for up to 20 hours a day. So don't worry if your brand new kitten sleeps a lot. This is perfectly normal.

Don't wake me up!
I'm having the best dream...

I don't care where I sleep!

ZZZ...

Kittens sleep in the strangest places. They have been spotted on top of computers, inside big furry boots, on piles of books, on top of dogs, next to the radiator, in boxes, on roofs... Where does *your* kitten sleep?

THE BEST PLACE OF ALL...

...is your lap, of course! It's warm and cosy and the perfect place for a kitten to nap. If a kitten does choose to snooze on your lap, it's a huge compliment. They will only sleep on a person they trust.

★ ★ ★ ★ ★ **TIME FOR A NAP** ★ ★ ★ ★ ★

Your kitten friend is fast asleep... again! See if you can wake it up!

OOPS... POOPS!

There's something a bit whiffy that kittens do and that's poop - a lot. (You can't blame them. They eat four meals a day after all.) So how *do* they learn to poop in the litter tray and not in the middle of your mum's best rug...?

Yes, of course I know what it's for. Can we go and play now?

SUPER POOPERS

Kittens are top of the class when it comes to litter training. They learn where to 'go' in no time! (They don't really like pooping on a rug anyway. Cat litter, sand or soil is wayyy better.) As soon as possible, simply pick up your kitten by the scruff of their neck – just like a mother cat does – and pop them into the litter tray. They'll soon work out why they are there.

SQUEAKY CLEAN

Did you know that cats spend half of the time they're awake cleaning themselves? They really do! There are a few reasons for this – licking cools cats down, it helps wounds to heal faster and it helps them to relax. But perhaps the most important reason is that by staying super duper clean, their enemies won't be able to sniff them out!

TEACH YOUR KITTEN

★ ★ ★ ★ ★   ★ ★ ★ ★ ★

It's toilet time! Help your kitten learn to use the litter tray.

HIDE-AND-SEEK

Help! Your super-cute kitten has vanished... Phew! It's under the kitchen table. Kittens just love to hide themselves away in the most unlikely places. Perhaps they just want to be alone? Maybe they want somewhere dark and cosy for a snooze. So whenever you think your kitten is lost, check out the washing basket...

Exploring is what I love the most!

A BRAND NEW WORLD

When they are very young, kittens need to stay inside. There, they are super safe from harm. But once they are 13 weeks old – and have had their vaccinations – it's time to unlock the cat flap and watch them leap, climb, run, jump and balance as they explore and find out all about the great outdoors.

I can see you!

HOURS OF FUN

How do you stop your tiny pet from feeling bored? Simple! Give them a cardboard box to play with. They'll absolutely love getting into it and out of it and into it again. And if they suddenly feel like a quick snooze, it's a wonderful place for your kitten to snuggle down. Zzz...

★ ★ ★ ★ ★ **PEEKABOO!** ★ ★ ★ ★ ★

Where's that kitten hiding? Keep an eye out, and you might just spot it!

Where are you?

Peekaboo!

CUTEST KITTY

 Kittens are much too cute and cuddly to visit big, scary theme parks or adventure playgrounds. (Kittens and zip wires don't really mix.) But if there are cool things to play with at home, they'll have just as much fun.

I'm going to knock this over!

BUILDING BLOCKS

Kittens can't resist knocking things over. It's not a good idea to let them play with anything breakable in case they hurt themselves, but wooden blocks are perfect. Stack blocks and watch your clever kitty knock them down again and again!

GREAT GAMES

⭐⭐⭐⭐⭐

Play with your kitten – it loves having so much fun!

> I haven't had so much fun since I last climbed the curtains!

UP TO SCRATCH

Kittens scratch to show other animals this is *their* territory. So there. It's also a great way for them to stretch their muscles. If you want to stop kittens scratching the furniture, it's a good idea to give them a scratching post to claw at instead. Then they can scratch and climb to their hearts' content.

MEOW!

 Kittens don't just meow. They purr. They hiss. Sometimes, they even trill like a telephone. But what do these sounds mean? Read on to find out what your brand new kitten is really saying!

KITTENSPEAK

If your kitten meows, it's trying to get your attention. Quick, stroke it! And if that doesn't work, give it a yummy snack. When a kitten trills, it's in the mood to hunt, so might like a mouse toy to play with. Or if you have a garden, your kitten might want to go exploring!

MEOW!

KITTEN NOISES

Have you noticed how kittens growl and hiss sometimes? It could be because something is upsetting them, so if you fix the problem, your kitten will love you for ever. There are no prizes for guessing what a kitten means when it sits on your lap and purrs – it's VERY, VERY HAPPY INDEED. Awwww.

★★★★★ **SING ALONG** ★★★★★

Choose a song or just play the keyboard, and your kitten will sing along with you.

BEST FRIENDS

 Congratulations! You know exactly how to look after your brand new kitten. You know how to keep it happy, what to feed it and how to understand what it's saying. Now all that's left to do is play with your kitten using all the tips you've learned in this book!

A FRIEND FOR LIFE

Your kitten is growing day by day. And as it grows, the close relationship between you grows too. Have you noticed how your kitten waits by the door when you come home or how it purrs when it sees you? The kitten has so many ways of showing how much it adores you... It will be your friend for life!

I love you so much.

KITTEN LOVE

It's very easy to show kittens how much you love them. Make sure you look after them well, by keeping them well fed. (Don't forget to give them treats too!) If they have long hair, be sure to brush it. But, most importantly, play with them. Kittens love that most of all.

★ ★ ★ ★ ★ **PLAY TOGETHER** ★ ★ ★ ★ ★

Stroke or play with your very own kitten.

AMAZING KITTENS

Your kitten is officially the cutest EVER. So make sure to stick a big grin on your face, because you should feel very proud of yourself.

Your cutest kitten is just perfect.

A NEW FRIEND

Guess what? The fun doesn't end there! While your perfect pet is napping, turn back to page 6 and get ready to choose a brand new kitten! These kittens don't just have nine lives – you can create as many as you like! And each one of them will be your very own adorable bundle of fun!